SOLITUDE OF SELF

SOLITUDE
OF
SELF

ELIZABETH CADY STANTON

PARIS PRESS   *Ashfield, Massachusetts   2001*

This edition of *Solitude of Self* was originally printed in the Congressional Record, 1892.

Library of Congress Cataloging-in-Publication Data

Stanton, Elizabeth Cady, 1815-1902.
Solitude of self / by Elizabeth Cady Stanton. – 1st ed.
   p.   cm.
ISBN 1-930464-01-0 (alk. paper)
1. Women's rights. 2. Individualism. I. Title.

HQ1426 .S8 2001
302.5´4—dc21   2001021513

B C D E F G H I J

Paris Press dedicates this book to Mary Seymour Lucas.

PUBLISHER'S NOTE

November. The last edge of summer bumped up against winter. And just as heat and cold exist in Ashfield, Massachusetts, in that shape-shifting month, they existed for me as Elizabeth Cady Stanton's *Solitude of Self* was performed in the documentary film *Not for Ourselves Alone*. Frozen and on fire, I listened to Stanton's understanding of solitude and its integral relationship to self-reliance and equality.

Throughout *Solitude of Self*, Stanton asserts that we face our most challenging moments alone, and that it is the birthright of every person to be equally prepared for these moments — regardless of gender, race, religion, or wealth. If we are equally educated and equally trained on all fronts of life, then says Stanton, we can call upon our inner resources when we need them most.

In *Solitude of Self*, Stanton presents the story of a servant girl who decorates a Christmas tree for her employer's children and later discovers that among all the presents beneath the tree there is no gift for her. In despair, she spends the winter night in a field, weeping. When the newspapers discover her plight and publish the story, many people send the girl presents. But, Stanton observes, at the moment of the girl's deepest sorrow and disappointment, she is alone. This keen solitude accompanies all forms of crisis for young and old alike, and our tools of survival — as individuals and as a society — include the development of skills that foster self-reliance.

Elizabeth Cady Stanton believed *Solitude of Self* to be her greatest achievement. In January 1892, she delivered it to the House Committee on the Judiciary, to the Senate Committee on Woman Suffrage, and to the National American Woman Suffrage Association. In 1915, thirteen years after Stanton's death, the U.S. Congress reprinted the speech and mailed 10,000 copies around the world.

Though Elizabeth Cady Stanton worked side by side with Susan B. Anthony for nearly fifty years, she has been cast in history's shadows and is long overdue homage as one of the founders of the women's rights movement in the United States. It is my hope that this publication will join the other recent print and film efforts to bring Elizabeth Cady Stanton the recognition and respect she so deeply deserves.

— Jan Freeman

SOLITUDE OF SELF

The point I wish plainly to bring before you on this occasion is the individuality of each human soul; our Protestant idea, the right of individual conscience and judgment—our republican idea, individual citizenship. In discussing the rights of woman, we are to consider, first, what belongs to her as an individual, in a world of her own, the arbiter of her own destiny, an imaginary Robinson Crusoe with her woman Friday on a solitary island. Her rights under such circumstances are to use all her faculties for her own safety and happiness.

Secondly, if we consider her as a citizen, as a member of a great nation, she must have the same rights as all other members, according to the fundamental principles of our Government.

Thirdly, viewed as a woman, an equal factor in civilization, her rights and duties are still the same—individual happiness and development.

Fourthly, it is only the incidental relations of life, such as mother, wife, sister, daughter, that may involve some special duties and training. In the usual discussion in regard to woman's sphere, such men as Herbert Spencer, Frederic Harrison, and Grant Allen uniformly subordinate her rights and duties as an individual, as a citizen, as a woman; to the necessities of these incidental relations, some of which a large class of women may never assume. In discussing the sphere of man we do not decide his rights as an individual, as a citizen, as a man by his duties as a father, a husband, a brother, or a son, relations some of which he may never fill. Moreover he would be better fitted for these very relations and whatever special work he might choose to do to earn his bread by the complete development of all his faculties as an individual.

Just so with woman. The education that will fit her to discharge the duties in the largest sphere of human usefulness will best fit her for whatever special work she may be compelled to do.

The isolation of every human soul and the necessity of self-dependence must give each individual the right to choose his own surroundings.

The strongest reason for giving women all the opportunities for higher education, for the full development of her faculties, forces of mind and body; for giving her the most enlarged freedom of thought and action; a complete emancipation from all forms of bondage, of custom, dependence, superstition; from all the crippling influences of fear, is the solitude and personal responsibility of her own individual life. The strongest reason why we ask for woman a voice in the government under which she lives; in the religion she is asked to believe; equality in social life, where she is the chief factor; a place in the trades and professions, where she may earn her bread, is because of her birthright to self-sovereignty; because, as an individual, she must rely on herself. No matter how much women prefer to lean, to be protected and supported, nor how much men desire to have them do so, they must make the voyage of life alone, and for safety in an emergency they must know something of the laws of navigation. To guide our own craft, we must be captain, pilot, engineer; with chart and compass to stand at the wheel; to watch the winds and waves and know when to take in the sail, and to read the signs in the firmament over all. It matters not whether the solitary voyager is man or woman. Nature, having endowed them equally, leaves them to their own skill and judgment in the hour of danger, and, if not equal to the occasion, alike they perish.

To appreciate the importance of fitting every human soul for independent action, think for a moment of the immeasurable solitude of self. We come into the world alone, unlike all who have gone before us;

we leave it alone under circumstances peculiar to ourselves. No mortal ever has been, no mortal ever will be like the soul just launched on the sea of life. There can never again be just such a combination of pre-natal influences; never again just such environments as make up the infancy, youth, and manhood of this one. Nature never repeats herself, and the possibilities of one human soul will never be found in another. No one has ever found two blades of ribbon grass alike, and no one will ever find two human beings alike. Seeing, then, what must be the infinite diversity in human character, we can in a measure appreciate the loss to a nation when any large class of the people is uneducated and unrepresented in the government. We ask for the complete development of every individual, first, for his own benefit and happiness.

In fitting out an army we give each soldier his own knapsack, arms, powder, his blanket, cup, knife, fork and spoon. We provide alike for all their individual necessities, then each man bears his own burden.

Again we ask complete individual development for the general good; for the consensus of the competent on the whole round of human interests; on all questions of national life, and here each man must bear his share of the general burden. It is sad to see how soon friendless children are left to bear their own burdens before they can analyze their feelings; before they can even tell their joys and sorrows, they are thrown on their own resources. The great lesson that nature seems to teach us at all ages is self-dependence, self-protection, self-support. What a touching instance of a child's solitude; of that hunger of the heart for love and recognition, in the case of the little girl who helped to dress a Christmas tree for the children of the family in which she served. On finding there was no present for herself she slipped away in the darkness and spent the night in an open field sitting on a stone, and when found in the morning was weeping as if her heart would break. No mortal will ever know the thoughts that passed through the mind of that friendless child in the long hours of that cold night, with only the silent stars to keep her company. The mention of her case in the daily papers moved many generous hearts to send her presents, but in the hours of her keenest suffering she was thrown wholly on herself for consolation.

In youth our most bitter disappointments, our brightest hopes and ambitions are known only to ourselves; even our friendship and love we never fully share with another; there is something of every passion in every situation we conceal. Even so in our triumphs and our defeats. The successful candidate for the Presidency and his opponent each have a solitude peculiarly his own, and good form forbids either to speak of his pleasure or regret. The solitude of the king on his throne and the prisoner in his cell differs in character and degree, but it is solitude nevertheless.

We ask no sympathy from others in the anxiety and agony of a broken friendship or shattered love. When death sunders our nearest ties, alone we sit in the shadow of our affliction. Alike mid the greatest triumphs and darkest tragedies of life we walk alone. On the divine heights of human attainments, eulogized and worshipped as a hero or saint, we stand alone. In ignorance, poverty, and vice, as a pauper or criminal, alone we starve or steal; alone we suffer the sneers and rebuffs of our fellows; alone we are hunted and hounded through dark courts and alleys, in by-ways and highways; alone we stand in the judgment seat; alone in the prison cell we lament our crimes and misfortunes; alone we expiate them on the gallows. In hours like these we realize the awful solitude of individual life, its pains, its penalties, its responsibilities; hours in which the youngest and most helpless are thrown on their own resources for guidance and consolation. Seeing then that life must ever be a march and a battle, that each soldier must be equipped for his own protection, it is the height of cruelty to rob the individual of a single natural right.

To throw obstacles in the way of a complete education is like putting out the eyes; to deny the rights of property, like cutting off the hands. To deny political equality is to rob the ostracized of all self-respect; of credit in the market place; of recompense in the world of work; of a voice in those who make and administer the law; a choice in the jury before whom they are tried, and in the judge who decides their punishment. Shakespeare's play of Titus and Andronicus contains a terrible satire on woman's position in the nineteenth century—"Rude men" (the play tells us) "seized the king's daughter, cut out her tongue, cut off her hands, and then bade her go call for water and wash her hands." What a picture of woman's position. Robbed of her natural rights, handicapped by law and custom at every turn, yet compelled to fight her own battles, and in the emergencies of life to fall back on herself for protection.

The girl of sixteen, thrown on the world to support herself, to make her own place in society, to resist the temptations that surround her and maintain a spotless integrity, must do all this by native force or superior education. She does not acquire this power by being trained to trust others and distrust herself. If she wearies of the struggle, finding it hard work to swim upstream, and allows herself to drift with the current, she will find plenty of company, but not one to share her misery in the hour of her deepest humiliation. If she tries to retrieve her position, to conceal the past, her life is hedged about with fears lest willing hands should tear the veil from what she fain would hide. Young and friendless, *she* knows the bitter solitude of self.

How the little courtesies of life on the surface of society, deemed so important from man towards woman, fade into utter insignificance in view of the deeper tragedies in which she must play her part alone, where no human aid is possible.

The young wife and mother, at the head of some establishment with a kind husband to shield her from the adverse winds of life, with wealth, fortune and position, has a certain harbor of safety, secure against the ordinary ills of life. But to manage a household, have a desirable influence in society, keep her friends and the affections of her husband, train her children and servants well, she must have rare common sense, wisdom, diplomacy, and a knowledge of human nature. To do all this, she needs the cardinal virtues and the strong points of character that the most successful statesman possesses.

An uneducated woman, trained to dependence, with no resources in herself must make a failure of any position in life. But society says women do not need a knowledge of the world; the liberal training that experience in public life must give, all the advantages of collegiate education; but when for the lack of all this, the woman's happiness is wrecked, alone she bears her humiliation; and the solitude of the weak and the ignorant is indeed pitiable. In the wild chase for the prizes of life they are ground to powder.

In age, when the pleasures of youth are passed, children grown up, married and gone, the hurry and bustle of life in a measure over, when the hands are weary of active service, when the old armchair and the fireside are the chosen resorts, then men and women alike must fall back on their own resources. If they cannot find companionship in books, if they have no interest in the vital questions of the hour, no interest in watching the consummation of reforms, with which they might have been identified, they soon pass into their dotage. The more fully the faculties of the mind are developed and kept in use, the longer the period of vigor and active interest in all around us continues. If from a life-long participation in public affairs, a woman feels responsible for the laws regulating our system of education, the discipline of our jails and prisons, the sanitary condition of our private homes, public buildings, and thoroughfares, an interest in commerce, finance, our foreign relations, in any or all these questions, her solitude will at least be respectable, and she will not be driven to gossip or scandal for entertainment.

The chief reason for opening to every soul the doors to the whole round of human duties and pleasures is the individual development thus attained, the resources thus provided under all circumstances to mitigate the solitude that at times must come to everyone. I once asked

Prince Krapotkin, a Russian nihilist, how he endured his long years in prison, deprived of books, pen, ink, and paper. "Ah," he said, "I thought out many questions in which I had a deep interest. In the pursuit of an idea I took no note of time. When tired of solving knotty problems I recited all the beautiful passages in prose or verse I had ever learned. I became acquainted with myself and my own resources. I had a world of my own, a vast empire, that no Russian jailer or Czar could invade." Such is the value of liberal thought and broad culture when shut off from all human companionship, bringing comfort and sunshine within even the four walls of a prison cell.

As women ofttimes share a similar fate, should they not have all the consolation that the most liberal education can give? Their suffering in the prisons of St. Petersburg; in the long, weary marches to Siberia, and in the mines, working side by side with men, surely call for all the self-support that the most exalted sentiments of heroism can give. When suddenly roused at midnight, with the startling cry of "fire! fire!" to find the house over their heads in flames, do women wait for men to point the way to safety? And are the men, equally bewildered and half suffocated with smoke, in a position to do more than try to save themselves?

At such times the most timid women have shown a courage and heroism in saving their husbands and children that has surprised everybody. Inasmuch, then, as woman shares equally the joys and sorrows of time and eternity, is it not the height of presumption in man to propose to represent her at the ballot box and the throne of grace, to do her voting in the state, her praying in the church, and to assume the position of high priest at the family altar?

Nothing strengthens the judgment and quickens the conscience like individual responsibility. Nothing adds such dignity to character as the recognition of one's self-sovereignty; the right to an equal place, everywhere conceded; a place earned by personal merit, not an artificial attainment, by inheritance, wealth, family, and position. Seeing, then, that the responsibilities of life rest equally on man and woman, that their destiny is the same, they need the same preparation for time and eternity. The talk of sheltering woman from the fierce storms of life is the sheerest mockery, for they beat on her from every point of the compass, just as they do on man, and with more fatal results, for he has been trained to protect himself, to resist, to conquer. Such are the facts in human experience, the responsibilities of individual sovereignty. Rich and poor, intelligent and ignorant, wise and foolish, virtuous and vicious, man and woman, it is ever the same, each soul must depend wholly on itself.

Whatever the theories may be of woman's dependence on man, in the supreme moments of her life he cannot bear her burdens. Alone she goes to the gates of death to give life to every man that is born into the world. No one can share her fears, no one can mitigate her pangs; and if her sorrow is greater than she can bear, alone she passes beyond the gates into the vast unknown.

From the mountain tops of Judea, long ago, a heavenly voice bade His disciples, "Bear ye one another's burdens," but humanity has not yet risen to that point of self-sacrifice; and if ever so willing, how few the burdens are that one soul can bear for another. In the highways of Palestine; in prayer and fasting on the solitary mountain top; in the Garden of Gethsemane; before the judgment seat of Pilate; betrayed by one of His trusted disciples at His last supper; in His agonies on the cross, even Jesus of Nazareth, in these last sad days on earth, felt the awful solitude of self. Deserted by man, in agony he cries, "My God! My God! why hast Thou forsaken me?" And so it ever must be in the conflicting scenes of life, in the long, weary march, each one walks alone. We may have many friends, love, kindness, sympathy, and charity to smooth our pathway in everyday life, but in the tragedies and triumphs of human experience each mortal stands alone.

But when all artificial trammels are removed, and women are recognized as individuals, responsible for their own environments, thoroughly educated for all positions in life they may be called to fill; with all the resources in themselves that liberal thought and broad culture can give; guided by their own conscience and judgment; trained to self-protection by a healthy development of the muscular system and skill in the use of weapons of defense, and stimulated to self-support by a knowledge of the business world and the pleasure that pecuniary independence must ever give; when women are trained in this way they will, in a measure, be fitted for those hours of solitude that come alike to all, whether prepared or otherwise. As in our extremity we must depend on ourselves, the dictates of wisdom point to complete individual development.

In talking of education how shallow the argument, that each class must be educated for the special work it proposes to do, and all those faculties not needed in this special walk must lie dormant and utterly wither for want of use, when, perhaps, these will be the very faculties needed in life's greatest emergencies. Some say, Where is the use of drilling girls in the languages, the sciences, in law, medicine, theology? As wives, mothers, housekeepers, cooks, they need a different curriculum from boys who are to fill all positions. The chief cooks in our great hotels and ocean steamers are men. In our large cities men run the bakeries; they make our bread, cake and pies. They manage the laundries; they are now considered our best milliners and dressmakers. Because some men fill these departments of usefulness, shall we regulate the curriculum in Harvard and Yale to their present necessities? If not, why this talk in our best colleges of a curriculum for girls who are crowding into the trades and professions; teachers in all our public schools, rapidly filling many lucrative and honorable positions in life? They are showing, too, their calmness and courage in the most trying hours of human experience.

You have probably all read in the daily papers of the terrible storm in the Bay of Biscay when a tidal wave made such havoc on the shore, wrecking vessels, unroofing houses, and carrying destruction everywhere. Among other buildings the woman's prison was demolished. Those who escaped saw men struggling to reach the shore. They promptly by clasping hands made a chain of themselves and pushed out into the sea, again and again, at the risk of their lives, until they had brought six men to shore, carried them to a shelter, and did all in their power for their comfort and protection.

What special school training could have prepared these women for this sublime moment in their lives? In times like this humanity rises above all college curriculums and recognizes Nature as the greatest of all teachers in the hour of danger and death. Women are already the equals of men in the whole realm of thought, in art, science, literature, and government. With telescopic vision they explore the starry firmament and bring back the history of the planetary world. With chart and compass they pilot ships across the mighty deep, and with skillful finger send electric messages around the globe. In galleries of art the beauties of nature and the virtues of humanity are immortalized by them on canvas and by their inspired touch dull blocks of marble are transformed into angels of light.

In music they speak again the language of Mendelssohn, Beethoven, Chopin, Schumann, and are worthy interpreters of their great thoughts. The poetry and novels of the century are theirs, and they have touched the keynote of reform in religion, politics, and social life. They fill the editor's and professor's chair, and plead at the bar of justice, walk the wards of the hospital, and speak from the pulpit and the platform; such is the type of womanhood that an enlightened public sentiment welcomes today, and such the triumph of the facts of life over the false theories of the past.

Is it, then, consistent to hold the developed woman of this day within the same narrow political limits as the dame with the spinning wheel and knitting needle occupied in the past? No! no! Machinery has taken the labors of woman as well as man on its tireless shoulders; the loom and the spinning wheel are but dreams of the past; the pen, the brush, the easel, the chisel, have taken their places, while the hopes and ambitions of women are essentially changed.

We see reason sufficient in the outer conditions of human beings for individual liberty and development, but when we consider the self-dependence of every human soul we see the need of courage, judgment, and the exercise of every faculty of mind and body, strengthened and developed by use, in woman as well as man.

Whatever may be said of man's protecting power in ordinary conditions, mid all the terrible disasters by land and sea, in the supreme moments of danger, alone woman must ever meet the horrors of the situation; the Angel of Death even makes no royal pathway for her. Man's love and sympathy enter only into the sunshine of our lives. In that solemn solitude of self, that links us with the immeasurable and the eternal, each soul lives alone forever. A recent writer says:

I remember once, in crossing the Atlantic, to have gone upon the deck of the ship at midnight, when a dense black cloud enveloped the sky, and the great deep was roaring madly under the lashes of demoniac winds. My feeling was not of danger or fear (which is a base surrender of the immortal soul), but of utter desolation and loneliness; a little speck of life shut in by a tremendous darkness. Again I remember to have climbed the slopes of the Swiss Alps, up beyond the point where vegetation ceases, and the stunted conifers no longer struggle against the unfeeling blasts. Around me lay a huge confusion of rocks, out of which the gigantic ice peaks shot into the measureless blue of the heavens, and again my only feeling was the awful solitude.

And yet, there is a solitude, which each and every one of us has always carried with him, more inaccessible than the ice-cold mountains, more profound than the midnight sea; the solitude of self. Our inner being, which we call ourself, no eye nor touch of man or angel has ever pierced. It is more hidden than the caves of the gnome; the sacred adytum of the oracle; the hidden chamber of Eleusinian mystery, for to it only omniscience is permitted to enter.

Such is individual life. Who, I ask you, can take, dare take, on himself the rights, the duties, the responsibilities of another human soul?

CHRONOLOGY

1815   Born to Judge Daniel Cady and
        Margaret Livingston in Johnstown, N.Y.

Elizabeth's earliest memory is at the age of four when a visitor declares, "what a pity it is that she's a girl!" after her sister Catherine is born.

1826   Death of her brother Eleazer.

Elizabeth is determined to become as educated as possible to comfort her grieving father, whom she recalls saying, "Oh, my daughter, I wish you were a boy."

1831   Begins her three-year education at
        Emma Willard's Troy Female Seminary
        after completing her schooling at the
        coeducational Johnstown Academy.

Elizabeth's years at Johnstown Academy later influence her support of coeducation. At Troy Female Seminary, considered the finest educational institution available to women, Elizabeth studies philosophy, history, mathematics, and logic. After graduating, she uses her father's library to study legal and constitutional history.

1840	Marries Henry Brewster Stanton.	*Elizabeth meets Henry Stanton at the home of her cousin, the abolitionist Gerrit Smith. Stanton is known as a charismatic speaker for the abolitionist platform. Before marrying, Elizabeth demands that the word "obey" be removed from the wedding ceremony.*
1840	Meets Lucretia Mott in London at the first World's Anti-Slavery Convention.	*When the Convention refuses to admit women as delegates, Elizabeth and Lucretia Mott discuss the need for a woman's rights convention in the USA. Mott, an abolitionist and Quaker minister, becomes Elizabeth's life-long mentor.*
1842	Gives birth to the first of seven children (five sons and two daughters), born between 1842 and 1859.	*Elizabeth's life as a new mother increases her awareness of the inequality between the sexes. This awareness is heightened after the family moves from Boston, where Elizabeth experiences a rich cultural and social life, to Seneca Falls, N.Y., in 1847.*

1848	Plans the first woman's rights convention with Lucretia Mott, Martha Coffin Wright, Mary Ann McClintock, and Jane Hunt; and writes the *Declaration of Sentiments*.	*The convention takes place in Seneca Falls, with 300 women and men in attendance. Elizabeth bases the* Declaration of Sentiments *on the* Declaration of Independence, *and demands equality for women, including the right to vote — a right denied to all women around the globe. Frederick Douglass is among the 32 men and 68 women who sign the* Declaration.
1851	Meets Susan B. Anthony, marking the beginning of a lifelong friendship and political collaboration.	*Amelia Bloomer introduces the two women on a sidewalk in Seneca Falls. Of her relationship with Anthony, Elizabeth later states, "I forged the thunderbolts, she fired them."*
1854	Reads her address to the New York legislature at a woman's rights convention. Demands equal civil status, the right to vote, to sit on juries, to equal inheritance rights for widows, a wife's right to her own wages, and the revision of the marriage code.	*Elizabeth's determination to make marriage an equal legal contract for women and men (allowing women the right to divorce) divides members of the suffrage movement and alienates many men.*

1861	Attends anti-slavery meetings throughout upstate New York, insisting that President Lincoln support the abolition of slavery.	*Traveling with Susan B. Anthony, Lucretia Mott, Frederick Douglass, and others, she faces raging mobs. In response to her husband's concern, she returns home but joins the group again when they arrive in Albany.*
1862	Moves to New York City.	*The Stantons move after Henry Stanton takes a position in the Customs House. Elizabeth returns to Seneca Falls once, as a paid speaker.*
1863	With Susan B. Anthony, creates the Women's Loyal National League, dedicated to freeing the slaves and empowering women in the U.S.	*Before it dissolves a year later, the group collects 400,000 signatures, which are used to help ratify the 13th Amendment, ending slavery.*
1865 – 1869	Opposes the exclusivity of the 14th and 15th Amendments, and alienates abolitionists, including Frederick Douglass, and many suffragists.	*During this period, Elizabeth realizes that the suffragists' efforts to abolish slavery did not ensure the abolitionists' support of woman's right to vote. In response, Elizabeth makes numerous racist comments in her speeches supporting woman's rights. When the Eleventh National Woman Rights Convention is held after the Civil War, many*

earlier supporters do not attend. Among the participants who do attend is Sojourner Truth, who stays with the Stantons in their home.

1868   With Susan B. Anthony, starts the suffragist newspaper *Revolution* and forms the National Woman Suffrage Association (NWSA).

Elizabeth becomes the first president of the NWSA. Lucy Stone spearheads the split between pro- and anti-15th Amendment suffragists and forms the American Woman Suffrage Association in 1869.

1870's For approximately eight months of the year, travels throughout the country, lecturing on woman's rights and earning her own money to support her family.

She joins the lyceum circuit, which employs entertainers and educators, and lectures once a day. Elizabeth's humor, wisdom, candor, and her maternal appearance make her an extremely popular speaker.

1876   Writes the *Declaration of Rights of the Women of the United States* for the U.S. Centennial celebration in Philadelphia. The NWSA is denied the opportunity to join the Centennial ceremony.

Ignoring the absence of an invitation, Anthony delivers a copy of Elizabeth's speech to the Centennial chairman in Independence Hall, and then presents the Declaration *from a bandstand outside.*

1881	Publishes the first volume of *The History of Woman Suffrage* with Susan B. Anthony and Matilda Joslyn Gage.	*After completing the second volume, she travels to Europe with her daughter Harriot. Several months later, Susan B. Anthony joins Elizabeth in London. When the two return to the U.S., they resume their work and the third volume is published in 1886.*
1887	Henry Stanton dies while she is visiting her daughter in England.	*Elizabeth discovers that her status as a widow permits independence and self-reliance.*
1890	Elected president of the National American Woman Suffrage Association (NAWSA), a merging of the National and the American Woman Suffrage Associations.	*As president, Elizabeth encourages the acceptance of all "types and classes, races and creeds" of women, and she urges that members address all issues that affect the lives of women.*
1892	Presents her last speech, *Solitude of Self,* to the House Committee on the Judiciary, to the Senate Committee on Woman Suffrage, and to the NAWSA before resigning as president.	*Elizabeth considers this to be her greatest speech. After her resignation, Anthony becomes president of the National American Woman Suffrage Association.*

1895	Publishes *The Woman's Bible*.	*In* The Woman's Bible, *Elizabeth interprets traditional biblical texts that promote the inferiority of women. Members of the NAWSA vote Elizabeth out of the organization. Susan B. Anthony attempts to dissuade the membership from doing so, but fails.*
1898	Publishes her autobiography, *Eighty Years and More*.	*Elizabeth dedicates the book to "Susan B. Anthony, my steadfast friend for half a century."*
1902	Dies at the home she shared with her son and daughter in New York City.	*Elizabeth recognized that it was unlikely that she would live to see women casting their votes at the polls. Years earlier, she wrote in her journal: "I never forget we are sowing winter wheat, which the coming spring will see sprout, and other hands than ours will reap and enjoy."*
1920	Congress adopts the 19th Amendment, granting women nationwide the right to vote.	

PARIS PRESS is a young nonprofit press publishing the work of women writers who have been neglected or misrepresented by the literary world. Publishing one to two books a year, the Press values work that is daring in style and in its courage to speak truthfully about society, culture, history, and the human heart. Paris Press relies on support from organizations and individuals. To send a tax-deductible contribution or to request a catalog, please write to *Paris Press, P.O. Box 487, Ashfield, MA 01330*.

Paris Press extends heartfelt thanks to the Massachusetts Cultural Council and to the many individuals whose generosity and assistance made the publication of Solitude of Self *possible. We are indebted to the support of Sally Montgomery and Anne Goldstein, to the advice of Patricia G. Holland and Joyce A. Berkman, and to the hard work of Jenna Evans. We offer special thanks to Tzivia Gover, who inspired this project, and to Ann R. Stokes, for her generosity. Immeasurable gratitude to Judythe Sieck for her beautiful design. And thanks also to Sally Morse Majewski and Hancock Shaker Village for permitting Paris Press to reproduce Hannah Cohoon's "The Tree of Light or Blazing Tree" on the cover of this book.*

The text of this book was set in Requiem, a typeface based upon the work of Arrighi (c. 1480-1527).

Design and composition by Judythe Sieck.

The painting on the cover is "The Tree of Light or Blazing Tree," 1845, by Hannah Cohoon. Ink and tempera on paper, 18 1/8 x 22 1/4 inches. Reprinted with permission from the Shaker Community, Inc., Hancock Shaker Village, Hancock, Massachusetts.